JOURNEY AROUND THE WORLD

ACTIVITIES TO DEVELOP GEOGRAPHY & SOCIAL STUDIES SKILLS

Written by Charlotte S. Jaffe and Anne Young
Cover Illustrated by Karen Sigler
Text Illustrated by Tracy Blecha

ISBN 0-910857-05-9

Exclusive Distributor: Educational Impressions, Inc.

Printed in the U.S.A.

EDUCATIONAL IMPRESSIONS, INC.
Hawthorne, New Jersey 07507

To the Teacher

The activities that follow are a challenging and fun way to have your students study the countries of the world and share their knowledge with parents, students, and community. The lessons may be used with gifted learners in pull-out or self-contained programs or with students in regular classrooms.

The book is written in an outline-type format that guides the students in selecting a country of interest and in completing an independent research project. A special feature of the book is the Creative Thinking Section, which provides many opportunities for the students to develop higher-level thinking skills. Based on Bloom's Taxonomy and Williams' Model, skills such as fluent thinking, flexible thinking, originality, risk taking, analysis and evaluation are stressed.

Section I: Map Skills

This section contains introductory map-skill activities. Teachers may supplement this information by allowing the students to explore classroom maps and globes. The students should have a basic knowledge of world geography before starting their "Journey Around the World."

Section II: Research Skills

The activities in this section provide basic guidelines that enable students to organize and develop their research skills. Teachers should provide opportunities for students to examine school and community resources. The SELECTION SHEET asks the students to make three study choices and to indicate their choices by first, second, and third preferences. This is done to avoid duplication of choices so that the International Festival will have more varied representation. The RESEARCH SHEETS are to be kept in the students' folders and used to collect information. Students may add other shapes and categories for special research information. The research information on these sheets will be helpful to the students in a variety of activities throughout their "Journey Around the World." Most of the activities in this section are self-explanatory. The teacher may choose to have the students make a cardboard flag or map from their initial sketches on the activity pages. Their vocabulary chart may be enlarged on poster paper and displayed on a bulletin board. SEND A LETTER makes use of the information that is provided in the Reference Section of the book and teaches the students another method of obtaining information.

Section III: Creative Thinking Skills

The activity pages in this section challenge the students to use their imaginations as well as make decisions and solve problems. The skills are open-ended and the teacher may select the activities that are best suited to the level of the class. Students may work independently or cooperatively on these activities.

Section IV: International Festival

The International Festival or Fair is the exciting culmination of the students' "Journey Around the World." The activities in this section provide step-by-step preparation for the Fair. Teachers may choose to include any or all of the activities. Parents and students from other classes may be invited to view the results of the students' efforts. Included in this section are thank-you notes, a certificate of participation, and an evaluation form.

Section V: Reference Materials

The Reference Section contains many handy resources that can be utilized throughout the "Journey." For example, there is a list of embassy addresses to which the children can write for information. Examples of handout materials which can be developed by the students are also provided. There are also instructions for a simulation game format for these activities. A pretest is included in this section.

We hope you and your students have a pleasant journey!

Charlotte S. Jaffe and Anne Young

Table of Contents

SECTION I:
Map Skills

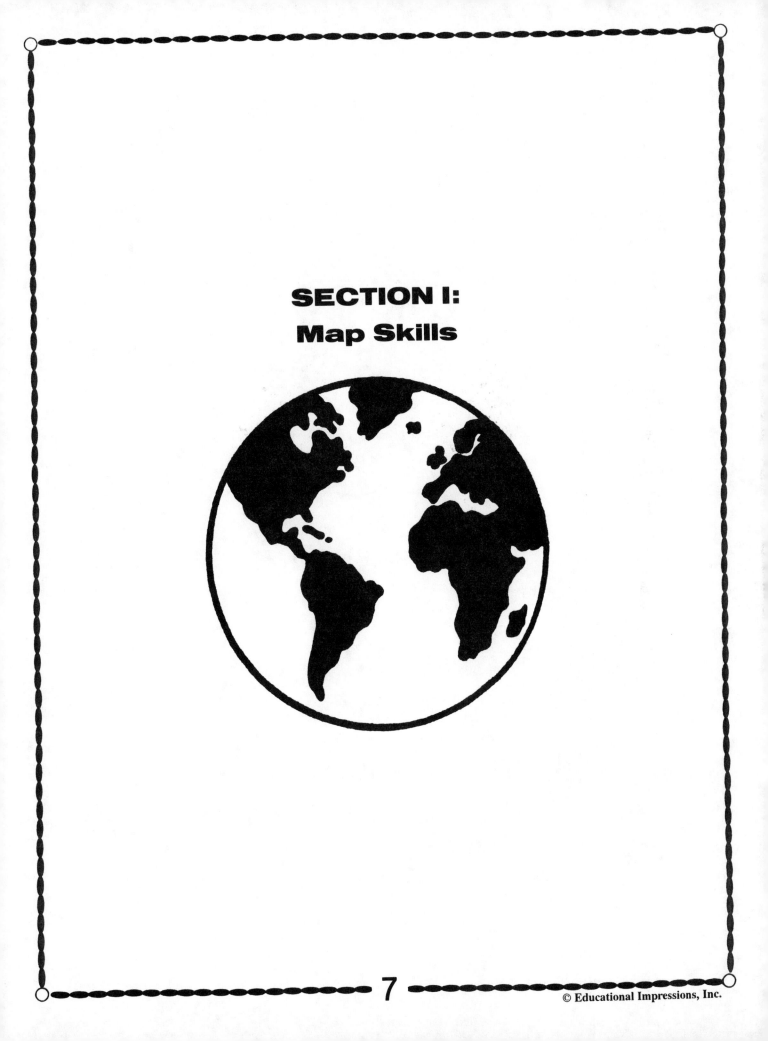

Map Skills
All About Our World

The world in which we live is so very interesting! It consists of large land areas called **continents** and large water areas called **oceans**.

There are seven continents: Africa, Antarctica, Asia, Australia, Europe, North America, and South America.

Using a world map or a globe, locate each of the seven continents. On which continent do you live? _____

There are four large oceans on our earth: the Atlantic Ocean, the Pacific Ocean, the Indian Ocean, and the Arctic Ocean.

Using a world map or a globe, locate each of the four oceans. Which ocean is the closest to where you live? _____

Map Skills
Be a Map Detective

As a map detective you will be searching for clues on a globe or a map. A globe is about the same shape as the earth. It is easy to see how the continents and the bodies of water are shaped. You can see from the globe that no part of the earth is really flat!

CLUE #1: LOOK FOR THE EQUATOR
Look for a line that is halfway between the North Pole and the South Pole. It circles the globe. The **equator** is called the **zero parallel**. It is the starting place for numbering the parallel lines that go around the globe. Each of the other lines has a number of degrees from 1 to 90. The symbol for degrees is a small circle (°). The lines also have a letter, N or S, to show if it is north or south of the equator. The equator line runs in an east-west direction.

CLUE #2: LOOK FOR THE PRIME MERIDIAN
Look for lines that run in a north-south direction. They are called **meridians**. They are numbered from 0° to 180°, and each has a letter, E or W. The **prime meridian** is located at 0°.

CLUE #3: LOOK FOR THE OCEANS OF THE WORLD
Find the four large bodies of water called **oceans**. They are the Atlantic Ocean, the Pacific Ocean, the Indian Ocean, and the Arctic Ocean.

CLUE #4: LOOK FOR THE CONTINENTS OF THE WORLD
Use a flat map to help you answer these questions about the seven continents.

1. What are the names of the continents? _____
_____

2. Which continents does the equator cross? _____
_____

3. Name the smallest continent. _____ The largest. _____

4. Which continents are crossed by the prime meridian? _____
_____

5. Which continent is located at 30° S and 130° W? _____

Map Skills
Take a Mystery Trip

First study the mystery trip described below and tell where you would go if you followed that itinerary. Then plan a mystery trip for your classmates by giving directions based on the lines on a world map.

Start at 30° S, 60°W.

Travel to 0°, 0°.

Travel to 30°E, 30°N.

Travel to 90°W, 30°N.

If you take this trip, where will you go? _____

_____

Use a map or globe to help you plan your mystery trip and to solve the ones created by your classmates.

11

Map Skills
Directions Can Be Fun!

There are four basic direction words that help us to read maps. They are NORTH (N), SOUTH (S), EAST (E), and WEST (W). They tell us directions on the earth.

A "compass rose" is usually on a flat map to show direction.

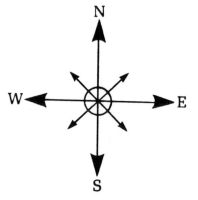

Fill in the missing directions below. Use **N** for north, **S** for south, **E** for east, and **W** for west.

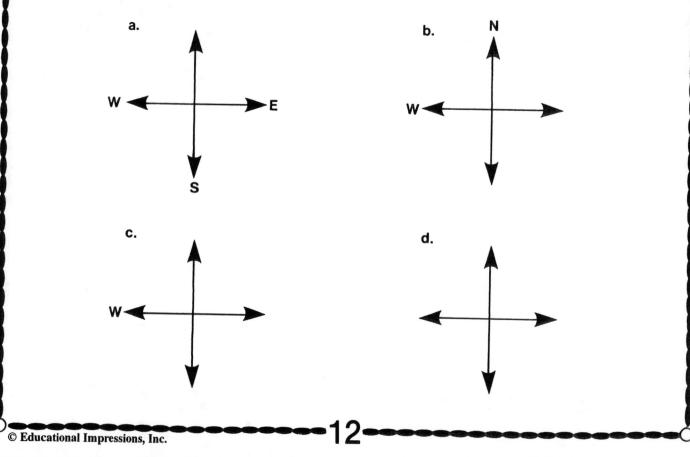

a.

b.

c.

d.

Map Skills
Map Comparisions

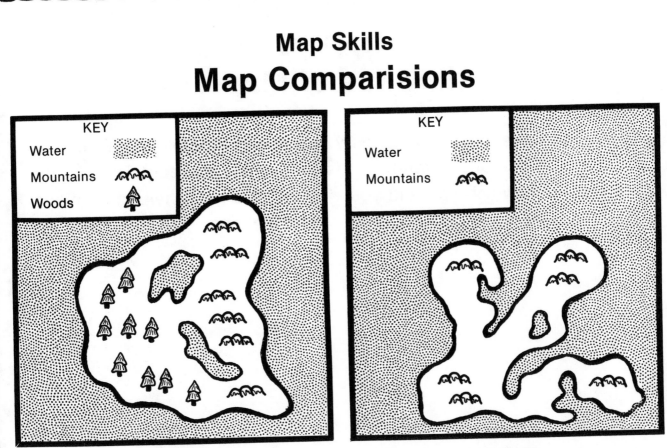

MAP A

MAP B

Look at the maps of the two imaginary countries above. How might you compare them? Size, shape, and geography are some considerations. Observe them carefully and then list the ways they are alike and different.

ALIKE	DIFFERENT

Map Skills
All Kinds of Maps!

Here is a brainstorming activity for you to complete! Within ten minutes, list as many different kinds of maps as you can! Think of the many ways in which you and your family have been helped by maps. After the time is up, circle your most unusual answer.

1.

2.

3.

4.

5.

6.

7.

8.

9.

10.

11.

12.

13.

14.

SECTION II:
Research Skills

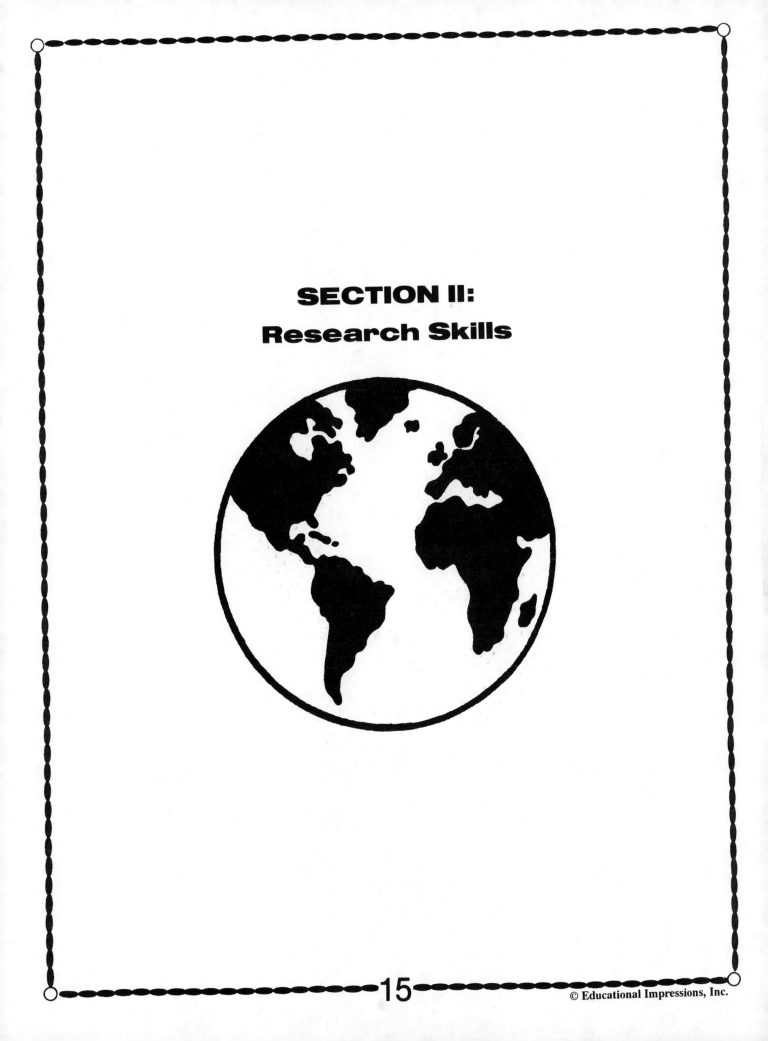

© Educational Impressions, Inc.

Selection Page

We are about to begin our journey around the world! Let's start at the beginning! We live in the town/city of _____, in the state of _____, in the country of _____, on the continent of _____. First you must decide on the country that you would like to research! Place a ✓ next to your first choice, put a ★ next to your second choice and put a • next to your third choice. Not every country could be listed on this page. You may add other choices to the list.

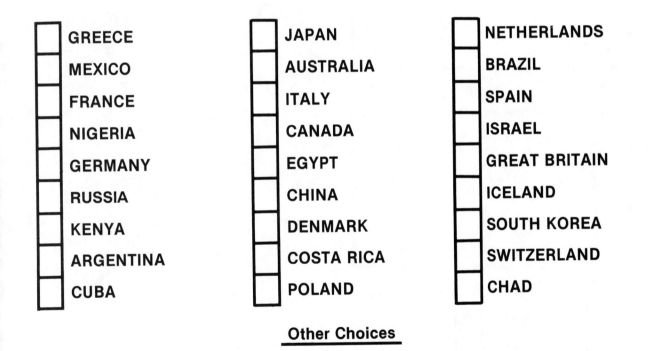

☐	GREECE	☐	JAPAN	☐	NETHERLANDS
☐	MEXICO	☐	AUSTRALIA	☐	BRAZIL
☐	FRANCE	☐	ITALY	☐	SPAIN
☐	NIGERIA	☐	CANADA	☐	ISRAEL
☐	GERMANY	☐	EGYPT	☐	GREAT BRITAIN
☐	RUSSIA	☐	CHINA	☐	ICELAND
☐	KENYA	☐	DENMARK	☐	SOUTH KOREA
☐	ARGENTINA	☐	COSTA RICA	☐	SWITZERLAND
☐	CUBA	☐	POLAND	☐	CHAD

Other Choices

Research Skills
Research Sheet #1

ALL ABOUT THE COUNTRY OF _____

LANDMARKS

By _____

RECREATION

CITIES

FOODS

FAMOUS PEOPLE

Research Skills
Research Sheet #2

ALL ABOUT THE COUNTRY OF _____

HOLIDAYS

By _____

IMPORTANT PRODUCTS

MOUNTAINS OR DESERTS

RIVERS OR LAKES

LANGUAGE

How do you say "hello"?: _____

Other important words:

Research Skills
Map Your State

Locate a map of your country in a reference book. Look carefully for rivers, cities, mountain ranges, and deserts. Copy the outline of your map in the space below. Add the names of the important cities and geographical features to your map. Be sure to mark the capital city with a star. After you have made your outline in pencil, go over it with crayon or marker. For an extra challenge, mount your map on heavy cardboard and cut it into jigsaw puzzle shapes. Exchange with your classmates and solve.

A Map Of

_____

Research Skills
Send a Letter!

In the Reference Section of this book you will find the names and addresses of Embassies and Information Offices of many nations. Find the name and address that will help you learn more about your research country and then write a letter asking for information. A sample letter is written below; however, you may compose your own in order to request the specific information you desire.

SAMPLE LETTER

910 Stephens Street
Cherry Hill, NJ 08034
December 10, 2000

Dear Sirs:

My name is Scott Peterson. I am in the fourth grade at the Andrews School. Our class is learning about the nations of the world. My assignment is the nation of Japan. Please send me maps, photographs, posters, or any other information that you may have available. I appreciate your help.

Sincerely,

Scott Peterson

Scott Peterson

Write your first draft of a letter in the space below. Then copy it over in good form on another piece of paper.

Research Skills
Make a Flag

A national flag is a great source of pride to the people of the country it represents. In many countries, popular stories explain how the flag originated. Americans tell the story of Betsy Ross and the first flag. In this activity you are asked to make a sketch of your research country's flag. Try to learn the meaning of the colors and symbols on the flag.

THE FLAG OF _____

HISTORY OF THE FLAG

_____
_____
_____
_____
_____
_____
_____
_____

Research Skills
Language Dictionary

Create a class dictionary! Along with your classmates, select ten or more common words or phrases to include in your dictionary. Each student will be responsible for adding his country's language. Duplicate the results! A list is started for you.

Word or Phrase	Mexico	France	Italy	(Etc.)
1. Hello	Hola			
2.				
3.				
4.				
5.				
6.				
7.				
8.				
9.				
10.				

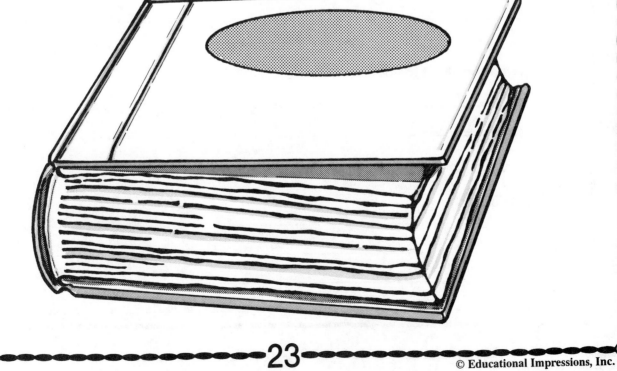

Research Skills
Famous People

Select a person from your research country who has made an outstanding contribution to his nation or to the world. This person may have achieved fame in politics, music, art, science, literature, or any other field. Look in the library for information about the person. Then use the following form to write your report. Share your findings with your classmates!

Name of famous person: _____

Date of birth: _____

Name of country: _____

Outstanding contributions: _____

_____

_____

_____

_____

_____

_____

_____

_____

Other information about the person's life: _____

_____

_____

_____

_____

_____

_____

_____

_____

Research Skills
Games Around the World

Do you like to play softball? tennis? hockey? Perhaps a game of dodgeball keeps you busy at recess time. Around the world, children enjoy different forms of recreation.

List at least 8 games and/or sports that are played in your own country and in your research country.

1.   5.

2.   6.

3.   7.

4.   8.

If the rules are different, explain on another sheet.

Describe a game or sport that is popular with the children of your research country. Write the rules of the game.

Name of Game or Sport: _____

Rules of Play _____

_____

_____

_____

_____

_____

_____

_____

On another sheet of paper draw a picture of the children of your research country playing this game.

Vocabulary Discoveries

As you are gathering information about your research country, you will discover many new words that describe your state in some way. These words may define special geographical features, cultural or recreational activities, or special kinds of homes or schools. Native clothing or food may be described by a new and unusual word. You are sure to uncover many such words in your research work. Write your vocabulary discoveries on the bottom of this page along with their definitions. When you have completed your list, share it with your classmates. Your teacher may wish to compile the words into a class booklet.

An example has been started for you.

Example:

HOLLAND

VOCABULARY WORD
polder

DEFINITION
An area of land that was once below water level and that has been reclaimed from the sea

COUNTRY: _____

VOCABULARY WORD   **DEFINITION**

Means of Transportation

Common forms of transportation are the automobile, train, airplane, and boat; however, there are also means of transportation that are found mostly in certain areas of the world. In Japan people still use the rickshaw to get from place to place. In England the double-decker bus is a common sight.

What usual and unusual methods of transportation are used in your research country? Draw a picture of the most unusual means of transporation in the box.

TRANSPORTATION IN THE COUNTRY OF _____

Research Skills
Find a Landmark

A landmark may be a famous building, structure, monument, or geographical feature that has special significance to the nation or to the area in which it is located. Choose a special landmark from your country to describe in this activity.

The special landmark is _____

It is located in the country of _____

Why is the landmark important? _____

_____

_____

_____

On another sheet of paper, draw a picture of your landmark. Combine your picture with those of your classmates and use them to make a collage or a bulletin board mural.

Research Skills
Shoe Box Scenes

Bring a shoe box, gift box, or small cardboard box to school. Create an imaginary scene of your country. Cut out a backdrop from travel folders or draw your own. Place clay or cardboard figures in the scene. Label the scene to show what is happening. In the space below, draw a sketch of your idea.

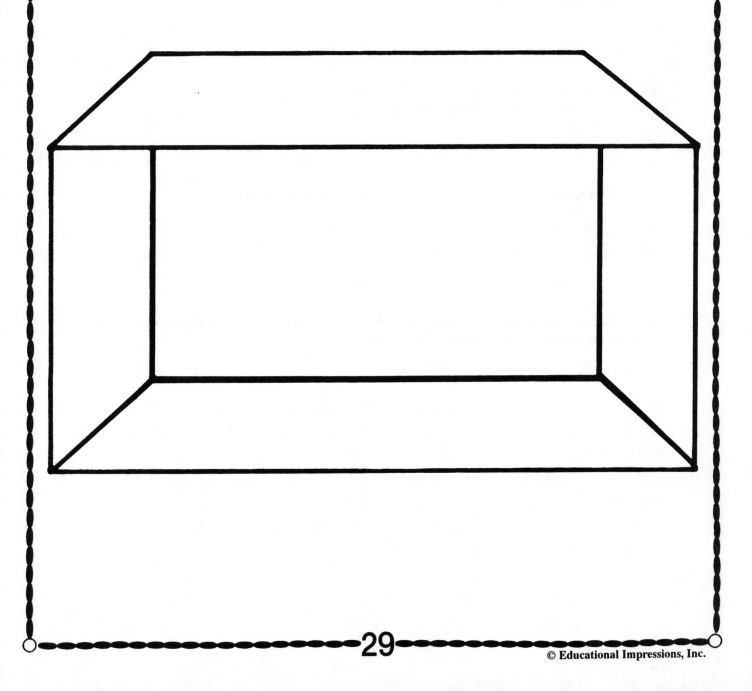

Research Skills
Currency Quiz

The form of money used by a country as a medium of exchange is called currency. Each country has its own basic unit of currency. For example, the basic unit of currency in the United States is the dollar.

Use the encyclopedia or other reference books to answer the following currency questions:

1. What is the basic unit of currency in Denmark? _____
   (Draw a picture of it in the space below.)

2. What is the basic unit of currency in Switzerland and Liechtenstein? _____

3. What is the basic unit of currency in England? _____

4. Which is used in China, the yen or the yuan? _____

5. What is the basic unit of currency in Austria? _____

Find the names of the currency used in the following countries and make a word find puzzle, a game or some other product with the information:

France _____   Mexico _____

Russia _____   Italy _____

Israel _____   Spain _____

Japan _____   Norway _____

England _____   Greece _____

Switzerland _____   Germany _____

Portugal _____   Sweden _____

You may add others if you wish:

_____   _____

_____   _____

Research Skills
Make a Bibliography

A bibliography contains a list of books or other materials (pamphlets, films, CD-ROM's, etc.) which were used to gather information—in this case, information about your country. Prepare your own bibliography in the space below. Use the category headings to help you organize it.

Name of Book	Author	Publisher	Copyright Date	Pages Used

SECTION III:
Creative Thinking Skills

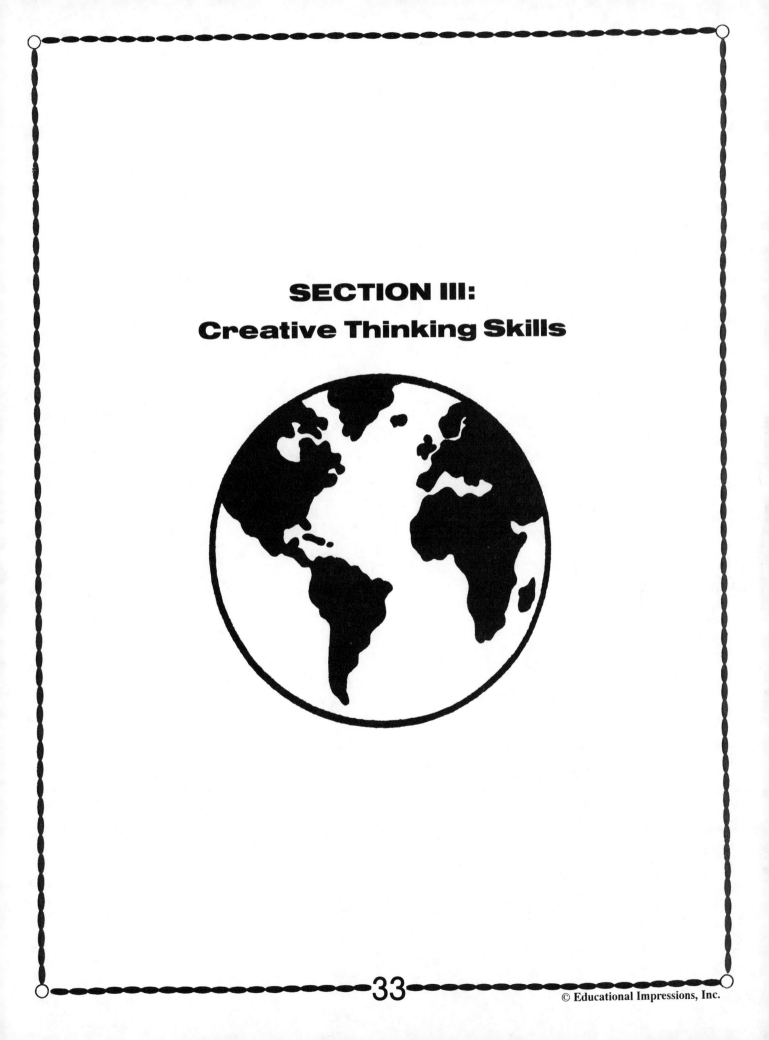

Creative Thinking
What Country Am I?

Here is a riddle about a country of the world. The first clue is GENERAL and the fourth clue is more SPECIFIC. Try to solve the riddle and then create two of your own! Share your riddles with your classmates.

CLUE #1: I am a country in Asia.
CLUE #2: Much of my land is covered with mountains.
CLUE #3: People get their food from the sea around me.
CLUE #4: The Tokyo Giants are a popular baseball team.

WHAT COUNTRY AM I? _____

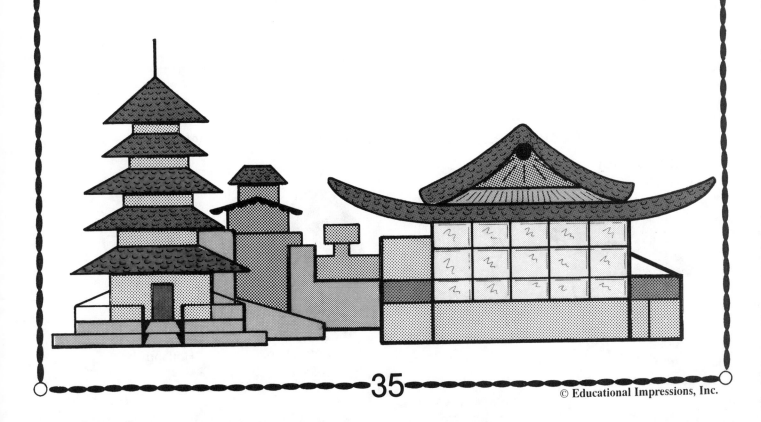

Creating Thinking
Pick a Pen Pal

It's fun to have a pen pal in another country. Choose one of the children pictured here to be your imaginary pen pal. What will you want to know about his or her life? What will you tell about yourself? (Don't worry about the translation!)

Dear _____,

_____

_____

_____

_____

_____

_____

_____

_____

_____

Your Pal,

_____

Now try to locate a real pen pal from another country. Write to him or her.

José
Mexico

Heidi
Switzerland

Soto
Japan

Wilhemina
Holland

Creative Thinking
A New Neighbor

Pretend that a child from the country of _____ has moved to your neighborhood recently. What are the main problems that he or she will have to face? What are the ways in which you might help your new neighbor overcome the problems? Write your ideas on the bottom of this page?

POSSIBLE PROBLEMS

1. _____

_____

2. _____

_____

3. _____

_____

4. _____

_____

5. _____

_____

HOW I CAN HELP

1. _____

_____

2. _____

_____

3. _____

_____

4. _____

_____

5. _____

_____

Creative Thinking
Create a Menu

If you went to your local restaurant, what would be your choice of food for breakfast? for lunch? for dinner? In this activity you must plan the menus for a restaurant in the country of _____. Be sure to choose some of the favorite foods of your research country. Give your restaurant a name!

_____ **RESTAURANT**

Breakfast   **Lunch**   **Dinner**

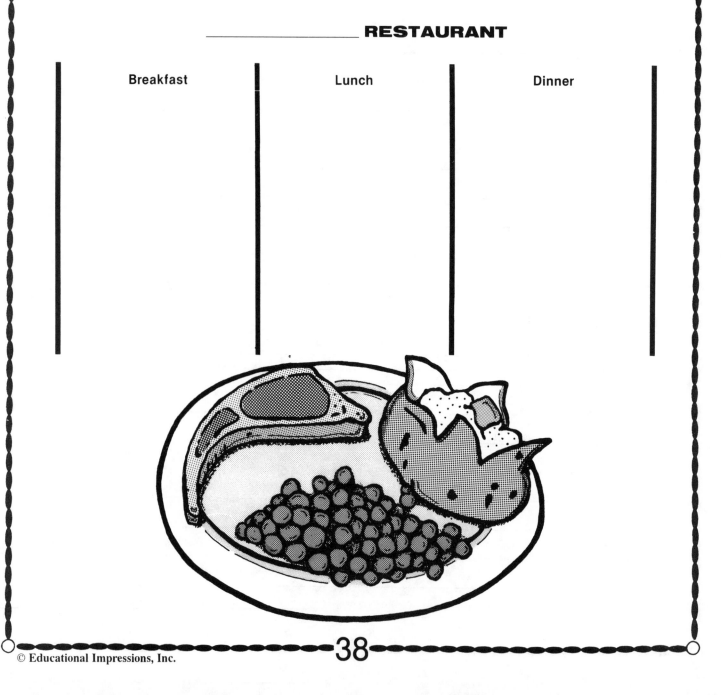

Creative Thinking
Create a Travel Poster

Pretend that you work for a travel agency. It is your job to design a travel poster that will attract tourists to the country of _____. Use your research information to help you plan your poster. You will want to include the outstanding attractions of the country. Arrange your poster creatively! Include the name of the country in it!

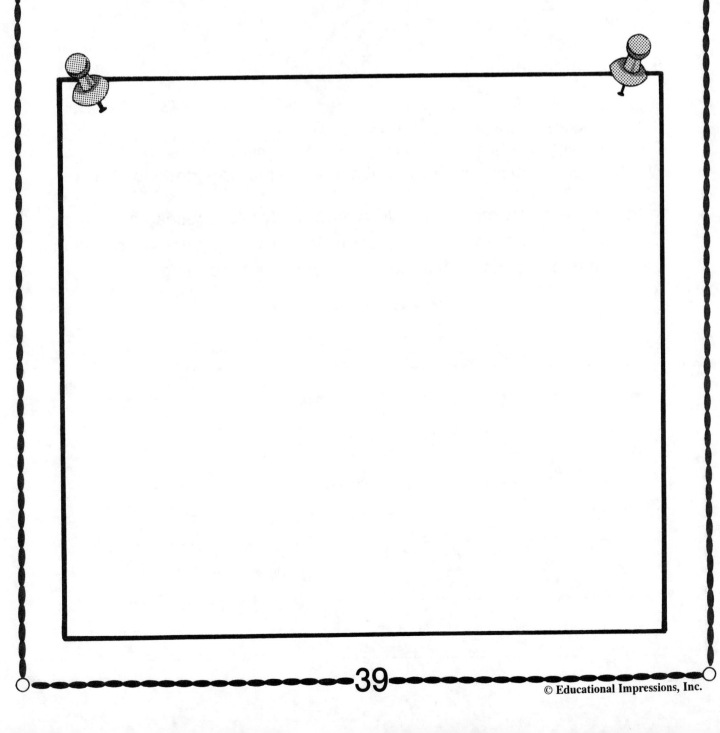

Creative Thinking
Make a Word Picture

Artists can create beautiful pictures with paint and brush! Writers can create beautiful pictures with words! Use your imagination and research information to create original word pictures of the country that you are studying.

Examples:

1. High, snow-capped mountains and clear blue lakes
2. A green island of low mountains, wide valleys and rich farmlands

Which country does each of the above word pictures describe?

In the space below create two word pictures for your research country. Then create four more for other countries of your choice. See if your classmates can guess which countries you are describing.

WORD PICTURES

1. _____

   _____

2. _____

   _____

3. _____

   _____

4. _____

   _____

5. _____

   _____

6. _____

   _____

Creative Thinking
Plan a Trip

Pretend that you are going to spend your next vacation traveling to the country of _____. Plan the route you will take and the different types of transportation that you will use. What special clothing or equipment will you need?

MY TRAVEL ROUTE

Starting Point: _____

Countries I Will Pass: _____

Bodies of Water I Will Pass: _____

Stops I Will Make: _____

Types of Transportation for Each Part of the Trip: _____

_____

SPECIAL CLOTHING AND/OR EQUIPMENT

1.

2.

3.

4.

5.

6.

7.

8.

Creative Thinking
Meet My Family

In this activity you must create an imaginary family that lives in the country of _____.

MY FAMILY

Family Name: _____

First Name and Age of Each Family Member:

_____

_____

_____

_____

_____

Name of Village, City or Town in Which the Family Lives: _____

Choose one family member and describe his or her experiences on a typical day. How are his or her activities like your own? How are they different?

_____

_____

_____

_____

_____

_____

_____

On the next page, draw a portrait of your imaginary family and a picture of the family's home.

Creative Thinking
Meet My Family

FAMILY PORTRAIT

FAMILY'S HOME

Creative Thinking
Classify the Countries

How many ways can you group the countries listed on this page? Consider the size, location, climate, geographical features, spelling, etc. There are many unusual possibilities. List your groupings and give each a title!

ITALY	**GERMANY**	**JAPAN**
NORWAY	**EGYPT**	**SWITZERLAND**
AUSTRALIA	**GREECE**	**SPAIN**
FRANCE	**GREAT BRITAIN**	**NEW ZEALAND**
ISRAEL	**KENYA**	**CHINA**
ICELAND	**MEXICO**	**RUSSIA**
INDIA	**CANADA**	**INDIA**

Example: ALL ARE ISLANDS

Japan

Australia

Iceland

Great Britain

New Zealand

Circle your most unusual group idea!

Creative Thinking
Hidden Countries Puzzle

Can you find the hidden countries in the sentences on this page? Each sentence contains the name of a different country. They are: Spain, China, Germany, France, Cuba, Denmark, America, Canada, Iran, Uganda, Chad, Poland, Ireland, and Kenya.

Underline your answers. The first one is done for you.

1. <u>Can a d</u>achshund do tricks?

2. She hurt her chin and cried.

3. Give your mother a hug and a kiss.

4. They bought flowers at the garden market.

5. Ron and I ran to the beach.

6. Fran celebrated her birthday on the fourth of July.

7. The mother bear found her lost cub and took him home.

8. His unfairness caused him to anger many people.

9. The doctor's needle causes pain but cures illnesses.

10. Ken yanked his sister's hair and made her angry.

11. The tire landed in the lake when it fell from the truck.

12. The peach added a sweet taste to the fruit salad.

13. Interpol and the CIA protect us from worldwide crime.

14. I am Erica and I am in the third grade.

Now create your own hidden country sentences. Write them on another sheet of paper and exchange them with your classmates to solve.

Creative Thinking
Job Search

Many occupations depend upon the geography, climate, natural resources or location of the country. For example, a ski instructor would likely find work in Switzerland; a fisherman would do well in Japan. In ten minutes, see how many occupations you can list that match the special environments of a particular country.

	COUNTRY	OCCUPATION
1.		
2.		
3.		
4.		
5.		
6.		
7.		
8.		
9.		
10.		
11.		
12.		
13.		
14.		
15.		

Creative Thinking
Create a Picture Postcard

Imagine that you and your family are visiting the country of
_____. Send a picture postcard to someone back in your
home town. Draw a picture of a special part of your trip on the picture
side. Describe your visit in words on the message side.

Draw Your Picture in the Box

Write the Message on the Left   **Write the Address on the Right**

Creative Thinking
If I Were a Child of _____

Pretend that you are a citizen of _____. Use your research information to help you compare your real life with that of a child of _____. How would your life change if you lived there? What things would be the same? Write your ideas in the space below.

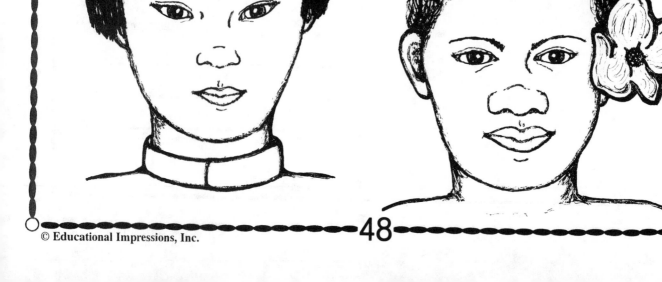

Creative Thinking
Hot Spot

Pretend that you are a news reporter for Worldwide Associated Press! It is your assignment to report on a fast-breaking story set in a foreign country of your choice. Create your event using real names of people and places. Remember to include the five W's and an H: who, what, why, when, where, and how!

Headline: _____

_____

_____

_____

_____

_____

_____

_____

_____

_____

_____

_____

_____

_____

_____

Creative Thinking
Categories Game

In fifteen minutes, try to fill in as many spaces as you can on the grid below. You may put more than one answer in each block. Try to think of answers that are unusual and you will score more points. A few examples are done for you.

	FOREIGN COUNTRIES	FOREIGN CITIES	FOREIGN RECREATION	FOREIGN FOODS
L				LASAGNE
A		ATHENS		
N	NETHERLANDS			
D				
S			SOCCER	

Score

1 point if someone else had same answer

2 points if you were the only one with that answer

Name _____

Creative Thinking
Alliterations Are Fun!

An alliteration is created by using the same sound at the beginning of consecutive words. Here are two examples:

Israel is interesting

Portugal pleases people!

Using country names, create your own alliteration sentences. Each sentence should contain at least three words. Try to use pertinent information in your sentences. You may also write some silly ones.

1.

2.

3.

4.

5.

6.

7.

8.

9.

10.

11.

12.

13.

14.

15.

Creative Thinking
Chart Your Answers!

Graphs and charts contain information that can be read quickly. One type of graph is called a **pictograph**. In a pictograph, pictures are used in place of numbers. Look at the example below. It charts the growth of world population. Each stick figure represents 500,000,000 people as shown in the key to the right.

PICTOGRAPH OF WORLD POPULATION

1900 👥👥👥
1910 👥👥👥
1920 👥👥👥👥
1930 👥👥👥👥
1940 👥👥👥👥👥
1950 👥👥👥👥👥
1960 👥👥👥👥👥

👤
500,000,000
People

Another type of graph is called the **line graph**. This type of graph can be used to show a great variety of facts. The example below shows the growth of world population. The line moves upward from 1900 to 1960 to show how the population increased during those years.

BAR GRAPH OF WORLD POPULATION

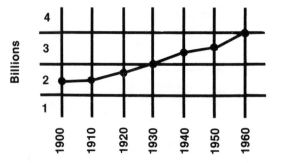

Both graphs measure growth every ten years. How much do you think the population grew in 1970? In 1980? Check your answers in a reference book.

Now create your own graph to show information! Use facts from your research about a country of the world or compare facts from several countries. You might want to show products, climate conditions, or population changes in cities or nations. Use any type of graph to illustrate your information.

Creative Thinking
A Different Point of View

Pretend that you are a child from your research country of
_____. Think of a counterpart for each of the items in the
column on the left and write your answers in the column on the right.

AMERICA   **COUNTRY OF** _____

1. Hamburgers _____

2. Baseball _____

3. Fourth of July _____

4. Jazz Music _____

5. George Washington _____

6. Statue of Liberty _____

7. Apple Pie _____

8. The White House _____

9. The Mississippi River _____

10. The Star Spangled Banner _____

11. The Empire State Building _____

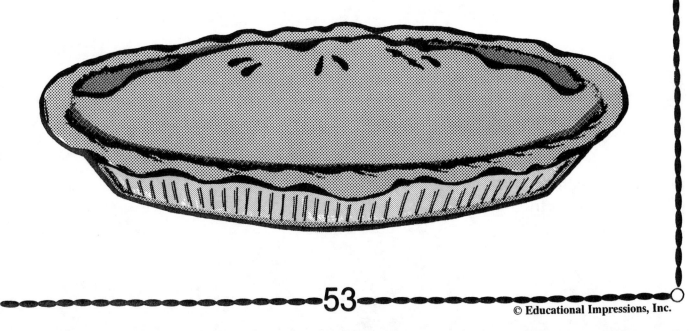

53

SECTION IV:
International Festival

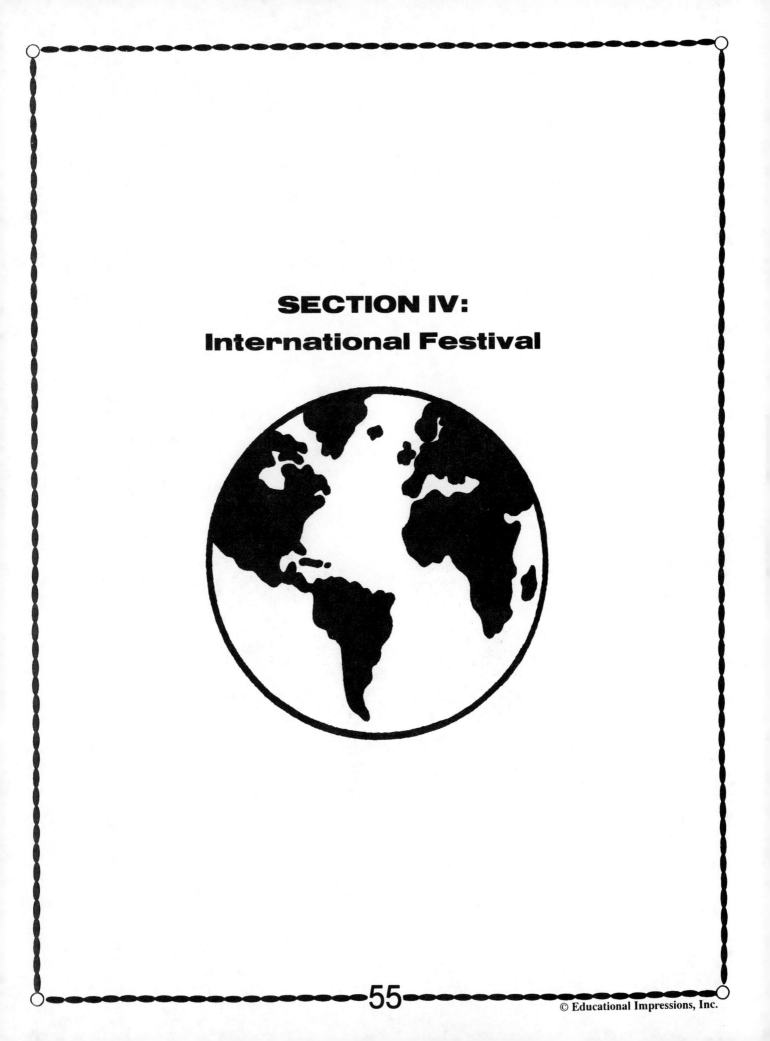

International Festival
About the Festival

In this section of your "Journey Around the World" you will use your decision-making, research, and creative-thinking skills to arrange an International Festival. The festival should be held in a library or in a classroom that is large enough to accomodate all of the displays. Each student should have his or her own table, and the name of each research country should be clearly and attractively marked. Maps, flags, foods, and posters may be displayed along with projects and handouts. Collected objects such as coins, stamps, dolls, toys and art objects will add to the completeness of your exhibit! Native songs, dances, and games may also be demonstrated as part of your display. Follow the activities in this section and use your own original ideas to make your exhibit at the International Festival a special one!

International Festival
Exhibit Planning Sheet

NAME _____

MY COUNTRY IS _____

DATE OF EXHIBIT _____

TIME _____ PLACE _____

THINGS I WILL NEED FOR MY DISPLAY:

_____ _____

_____ _____

_____ _____

_____ _____

_____ _____

A SKETCH OF MY DISPLAY:

International Festival
Share Your Knowledge

In preparation for the International Festival, you are responsible for making a handout that will show some of the information that you have obtained from your research. Look in the Reference Section of this book; it contains some ideas for handouts such as Language Dictionaries, National Songs, Recipes, and Pictures. Be creative and come up with an original idea! Duplicate your handout and share it with others on the day of the Festival! On this page, list some ideas that you might develop into informative handouts.

1.

2.

3.

4.

5.

6.

7.

8.

9.

10.

11.

12.

Circle your best idea!

International Festival
Research Chart

On this page you will find a research chart plan. Use this sample chart for your first draft. A larger copy of this can be placed on the front of your exhibit table with pictures highlighting various features of your study.

Use your research activity pages to discover as many important facts as you can about your country. You may add on extra lines for more topics.

RESEARCH CHART FOR THE COUNTRY OF _____

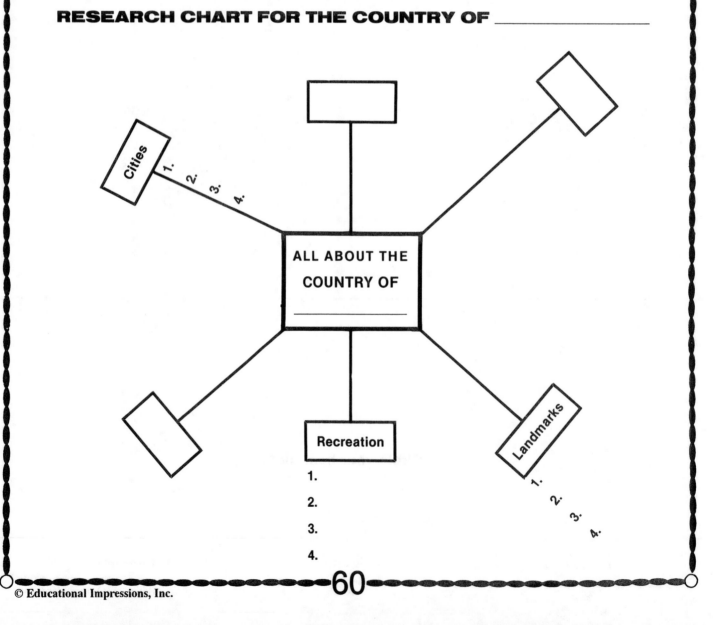

International Festival
Be a Speech Writer

A very important part of the International Festival will be the presentation of a short speech describing the highlights of your research country. You may choose to relate any facts that you think are important and that the visitors to the fair will find interesting. A sample speech might start...

"Hello! My research country is Mexico. Mexico is the southern neighbor of the United States. Spanish is the spoken language, and 'hola' means 'hello.'"

Compose your speech on the bottom of the page. Refer to your research sheets for ideas and information. Be sure to include at least six important facts in your speech.

International Festival
Create a Project

You might want to include a creative project on your exhibit table. The project should reflect the results of your research in some way. Here is a list of project ideas.

CLAY MODEL	TRAVELOG	FILMSTRIP
CREATIVE GAME	MOBILE	POEM BOOKLET
COLLAGE	MAP	BOOK
CARTOON BOOK	FLIP BOOK	PHOTOGRAPHY
BROCHURE	DEMONSTRATION	PROJECT CUBE
LEARNING CENTER	NEWSPAPER	ORIGINAL SONG
TAPE	RADIO SHOW	SLIDE SHOW
MURAL	MAGAZINE	COMMERCIAL
DICTIONARY	SILKSCREEN	COMPUTER PRINTOUT

On the bottom of this page, list some of your project ideas. Describe the information that they might contain. For example:

Project Idea	Type of Information
Creative Game: Race Through Brazil	Geography of Brazil

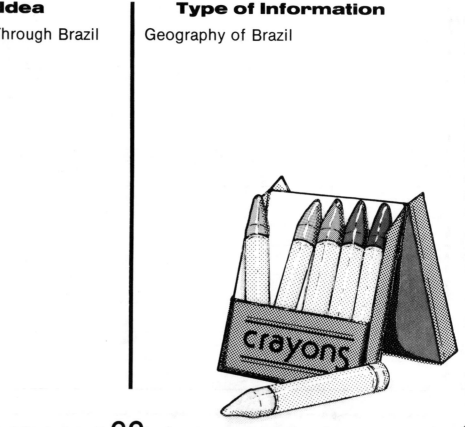

International Festival
About the Festival

Every country has some favorite foods that are popular as part of everyday meals and some that are eaten mostly on special occasions. Choose a favorite food from your research country to serve as part of your display.

NAME OF FOOD: _____

WHEN TYPICALLY SERVED:

RECIPE:

Draw a picture of the way your food will look when you present it.

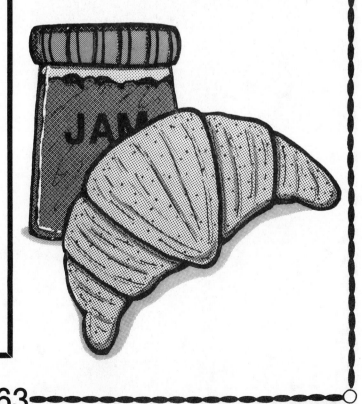

Dress Up for Your Country

List the kinds of clothing that are worn in your research country.

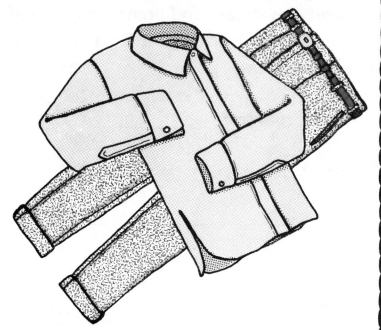

Wouldn't it be fun to wear something from your country at the International Festival? Draw a sketch to show what you will wear.

International Festival
Invitations

You may select either of the two invitation forms below to invite visitors to your festival or you may write your own.

YOU ARE INVITED TO OUR INTERNATIONAL FESTIVAL

DATE: _____

TIME: _____

PLACE: _____

WE HOPE THAT YOU WILL ENJOY IT!

LOVE,

_____

_____
_____
_____

Dear _____,

We would like to invite you to come to our International Festival. It will be held on _____ at _____ in _____.

We hope you will have a super time!

Love,

_____

International Festival
Thank You Note

Dear _____,

   Thank you for all of your help and cooperation in making our International Festival a big success! Our class really appreciates your efforts. We hope that you enjoyed visiting our fair and that your visit added to your knowledge of our world.

                                        Love,

                                        _____

                                        And Class

(Sign Class Names Below)

Certificate

This is to certify that

_____

has done an outstanding job with

_____ country exhibit

all about the country of

_____

Signed _____

Date _____

67

International Festival
Evaluation

This evaluation sheet may be duplicated and distributed to visitors as they complete their tour of the International Festival.

OUR INTERNATIONAL EXHIBIT

1. Which country did you enjoy learning about the most? _____

2. What new fact did you learn about this country? _____
_____

3. Name one special thing that you learned from attending the exhibit. ____
_____

4. Name some outstanding projects that you saw at the exhibit. _____
_____
_____

5. What was your favorite handout?_____
_____

6. Would you like to see another exhibit of this kind? _____

7. Do you have any suggestions for future exhibits?

NAME (Optional) _____ Date _____

SECTION V:
Reference Materials

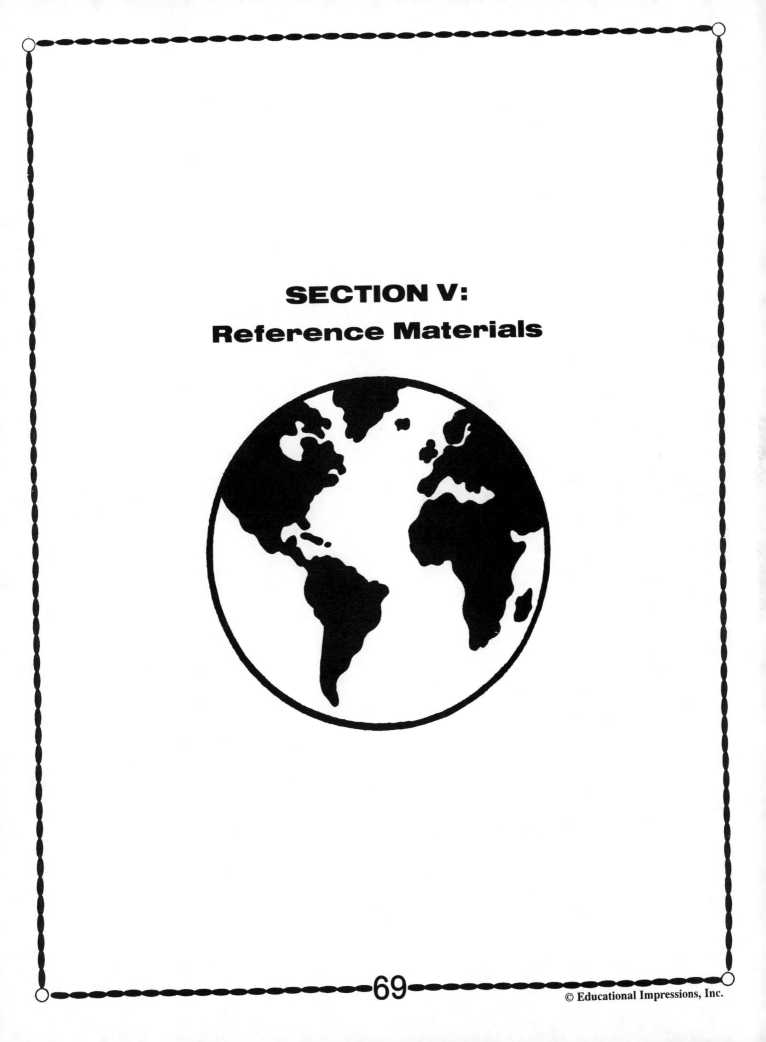

Reference Section
Pre-Test

1. Name the imaginary line that circles the globe and is halfway between the North and South Poles. _____

2. Name the four bodies of water called oceans.

_____

_____

3. Name the seven large land masses called continents.

_____

_____

4. Name one or more popular foods that are found in each of these countries:

Mexico: _____

France: _____

England: _____

5. Name one landmark of the U.S.A. _____

6. Name one landmark found in another country. _____

7. Name popular sports of America in the column on the left and those played mostly in other countries in the column on the right. _____

AMERICA	OTHER NATIONS
_____	_____
_____	_____
_____	_____
_____	_____

8. Name one of each of the following from a foreign country and name that country.

Currency: _____

River: _____

Mountain: _____

Holiday: _____

71

Reference Section
Simulation Game Instructions

1. A large world map with mileage equivalents should be placed on a classroom bulletin board before beginning the game.

2. Using the SELECTION PAGE, each student chooses a "Home Country." If the class is large, students may work in small groups.

3. Each student designs a marker that is symbolic of his country (landmark, product, etc.). This marker will be used to show each stop along the route. It can be pinned or taped to the map.

4. Students are required to complete activities from:

    > Section I: Maps
    > Section II: Research
    > Section III: Creative Thinking

    As students complete the activity pages they receive points which convert into miles.

5. SCORING is as follows. Each completed activity page is equal to 5 points or 250 miles; however, the teacher may deduct points if the product is unsatisfactory or add points if the product is superior.

1 point = 50 miles	6 points = 300 miles
2 points = 100 miles	7 points = 350 miles
3 points = 150 miles	8 points = 400 miles
4 points = 200 miles	9 points = 450 miles
5 points = 250 miles	10 points = 500 miles

6. The teacher may keep a record of each student's travel points on the SCORING SHEET. The sheet may be duplicated and placed on the bulletin board near the map.

7. Each student is required to use at least 5 different types of TRANSPORTATION during his journey. He must keep a record of the transportation used on the scoring sheet.

8. After 1,000 miles of travel, each student selects a DETOUR CARD. These cards may be duplicated and attached to heavy cardboard for classroom use. Students may create additional Detour Cards to be used in the game.

9. BONUS POINTS for extra credit projects may be awarded by the teacher. For example:

    > MODELS = 5 points
    > REPORTS = 5 points
    > CREATIVE STORIES OR POEMS = 5 points

10. The first student to travel around the nation is the winner of the game. The teacher may require all students to accumulate a minimum amount of points before ending the game and proceeding to the International Festival.

Detour Cards

EARTHQUAKE!

Many trees and wires are down. Do not move this turn. Conditions are dangerous!

SEVERE RAINSTORMS

Many trees and wires are down. You are unable to travel at this time. Miss this turn!

FLOODED ROADS!

Roads are flooded in all directions! You must go back 100 miles!

AIRLINE STRIKE!

There are no flights out of this stop today! You may travel 100 miles by land.

TRAFFIC VIOLATION!

Your vehicle was going the wrong way on the highway. Local police have stopped you! Travel only 25 miles this turn.

SHIP REPAIRS NEEDED

No water transportation is possible. You may travel 100 miles by land today.

VOLCANO DANGER!

A volcano is about to erupt! Go back 100 miles to be safe!

DENSE FOG

All transportation is halted today due to the weather. Miss this turn.

TYPHOON AHEAD!

Stay where you are for your own protection! Do not move this turn!

TRAINS DERAILED!

No travel by train is allowed today. You may use water transportation for 150 miles if possible.

LOST LUGGAGE!

Your luggage must be replaced at this stop! You must miss this turn.

BUS DRIVERS STRIKE!

All bus transportation is halted for today. You may travel 200 miles by air.

Reference Section
Detour Cards

OUT OF GAS
Your car ran out of gas on the highway. You will be delayed. Travel only 50 miles this turn.

BRIDGE COLLAPSED!
You must go back 25 miles!

AVALANCHE
All roads out are blocked! All airports are closed! You must miss this turn.

HAIL STORM!
You must wait for the storm to pass. Travel only 25 miles this turn.

ROAD BEING REPAIRED
There are detours in all directions. Go back 50 miles!

FENDER BENDER
You have witnessed a minor accident. You lose a lot of travel time. Proceed only 10 miles this turn.

SHIPWRECK!
Your ship is caught in a storm! Abandon ship! Travel 50 miles north when you reach land!

POLICE BARRICADE
The police are questioning everyone who passes. You may travel only 50 miles this turn.

BLIZZARD!
Record-breaking snowfall has brought all transportation to a halt! You may not travel this turn.

FLAT TIRE!
You must stop to fix your flat tire. Travel only 50 miles this turn.

ICY ROADS!
Travel is very dangerous. You may travel only 50 miles this turn.

PARADE!
A very long parade is blocking your passage. You must wait for it to pass. Travel only 100 miles this turn.

Reference Section
Scoring Sheet

JOURNEY AROUND THE WORLD

Student	Home Country	Points Accumulated	Miles Accumulated	Transportation	Last Stop

Handout Sample

COUNTRY AND CAPITAL
MATCH-UP

Match the countries on the left with their capitals in the column on the right. In the spaces provided, write the numbers which appear before the correct capitals. The first has been done for you.

COUNTRIES

_5_ United States
____ Japan
____ Spain
____ Israel
____ Argentina
____ Greece
____ Lebanon
____ Italy
____ Denmark
____ Canada
____ Bolivia
____ Russia
____ Chile
____ United Kingdom

CAPITALS

1. Santiago
2. Athens
3. Tokyo
4. Madrid
5. Washington, D.C.
6. Buenos Aires
7. Rome
8. Ottawa
9. London
10. Jerusalem
11. Copenhagen
12. La Paz
13. Moscow
14. Beirut

Now use the code to figure out the message. Write the letters which correspond to the numbers you filled in in part one of the activity. Be sure to keep them in the correct order. The first has been done for you.

1	2	3	4	5	6	7	8	9	10	11	12	13	14
L	M	T	S	I	S	L	W	D	A	L	O	R	A

I __ ' __ __ __ __ __ __ __ __ __ __ __ __!

Reference Section
Handout Sample

SPANISH
VOCABULARY SHEET

Me llamo:_____

La Fecha:_____

Buenos días
Good morning

Hola — Hello
Adiós — Goodbye

Buenos tardes
Good afternoon

Gracias
Thank you

Buenas noches
Good evening (night)

Hasta mañana
See you tomorrow

Hasta pronto — See you soon

Me llamo — My name is

¿Cómo estás? — How are you? (familiar)

Muy mal — Very poorly

¿Cómo está usted? — How are you? (formal)

Muy bien — Very well

¿Qué tal? — How's everything?

Así, Así — So, So

¿Dónde? — Where?

La fecha — The date

¿Qué es esto? — What is this?

Es — It is

Está bien — That's fine

No — No

Repita — Repeat

Si — Yes

Por favor — Please

Reference Section
Handout Sample

SWITZERLAND
SEEK-AND-FIND

```
A Q O P A N C A T T L E R K S K I B R T
C M R I J P Z Y F F R D L I Q B M I B T
H Z S T C E G K N O E P O R U E U W I O
E X V T T R A L V X B A T J X R L S S A
E F J D B I P S R X D I M A K N T X K Y
S L M A T T E R H O R N N N M B C P S I E
E O X Q P M T J L R X P M I T G K Y I C
Y R S U T D F A C Q P I L H Y S A P N L
T M L E H A E Y D H M E L Q S T P O G A
X A T T M O F R A N C R Y A L M N O A L
X P T A R C B Y H S A S L M A D C T Y V
K C D L H T A R W Y A L T Z X Q H P I L
E M F O C T I L O C D I R F E E N C T L
S Q I C L M A Z P R I X L E T S A M D O
X A T O A H I L P E O T Q M Z N Z C L I
R T S H A L I P M O N P L W A T C H E S
T R A C C D B H U Z V H A U I O I F C H
G M I A C D Q P R L P W O O R S A W I O
C R O Y Q M T I Z R I O I R Q U M I S C
H Q I S W I S S A L P S B C N I Z V S I
```

Alpenhorn	Franc	Cheese	Swiss Alps
Bern	Matterhorn	Chocolate	Switzerland
Cattle	Skiing	Europe	Watches

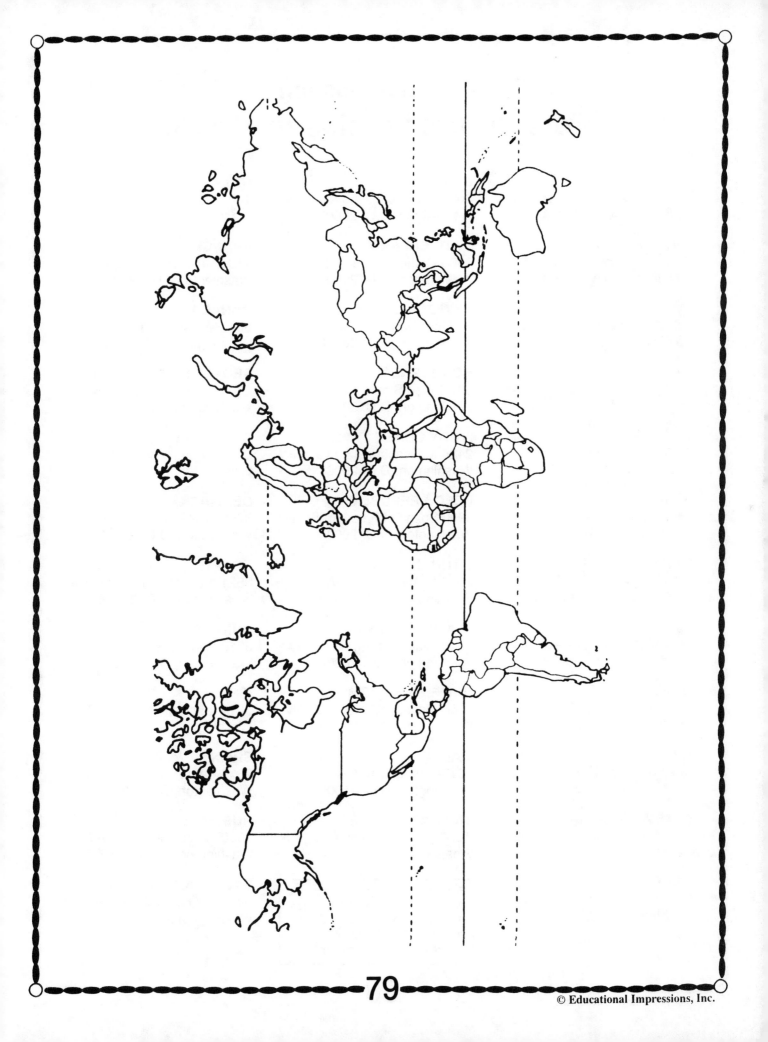

Research Section
Foreign Embassies in U.S.A.

PERU
1700 Massachusetts Ave., NW
Washington, D.C. 20036

SOUTH AFRICA
3051 Massachusetts Ave., NW
Washington, D.C. 20008

LATVIA
4325 Seventeenth Street, NW
Washington, D.C. 20011

ARGENTINA
1600 New Hampshire Ave., NW
Washington, D.C. 20009

URUGUAY
2715 M Street, NW, 3rd floor
Washington, D.C. 20007

MAURITIUS
4301 Connecticut Ave., NW
Washington, D.C. 20005

TUNISIA
1515 Massachusetts Ave., NW
Washington, D.C. 20005

MADAGASCAR
2374 Massachusetts Ave., NW
Washington, D.C. 20008

VENEZUELA
1099 30th Street, NW
Washington, D.C. 20007

SWEDEN
1501 M Street, NW
Washington, D.C. 20005

ZAMBIA
2419 Massachusetts Ave., NW
Washington, D.C. 20008

MEXICO
1911 Pennsylvania Ave., NW
Washington, D.C. 20006

BRAZIL
3006 Massachusetts Ave., NW
Washington, D.C. 20008

SWITZERLAND
2900 Cathedral Ave., NW
Washington, D.C. 20008

NEW ZEALAND
37 Observatory Circle, NW
Washington, D.C. 20008

HONDURAS
307 Tilden Street
Washington, D.C. 20008

IVORY COAST
2424 Massachusetts Ave., NW
Washington, D.C. 20008

CZECH REPUBLIC
3900 Spring of Freedom St., NW
Washington, D.C. 20008

LITHUANIA
2622 Sixteenth St., NW
Washington, D.C. 20009

STATE OF KUWAIT
2940 Tilden Street, NW
Washington, D.C. 20008

UNITED KINGDOM
3100 Massachusetts Ave., NW
Washington, D.C. 20008

MALTA
2017 Connecticut Ave., NW
Washington, D.C. 20008

IRELAND
2234 Massachusetts Ave., NW
Washington, D.C. 20008

For more listings, contact the Worldwide Chamber of Commerce, P.O. Box 1029, Loveland, CO, 80539-1029. A useful internet source is www.embassy.org.

ITALY
1601 Fuller Street, NW
Washington, D.C. 20009

FRANCE
4101 Reservoir Road, NW
Washington, D.C. 20007

CANADA
501 Pennsylvania Ave., NW
Washington, D.C. 20001

PEOPLE'S REP. OF CHINA
2300 Connecticut Ave., NW
Washington, D.C. 20008

COLOMBIA
2118 Leroy Place, NW
Washington, D.C. 20008

DENMARK
3200 Whitehaven Street, NW
Washington, D.C. 20008

EGYPT
3521 International Court, NW
Washington, D.C. 20008

HUNGARY
3910 Shoemaker Street, NW
Washington, D.C. 20008

ISRAEL
3514 International Drive, NW
Washington, D.C. 20008

SPAIN
2375 Pennsylvania Ave., NW
Washington, D.C. 20037

RUSSIA
2650 Wisconsin Ave., NW
Washington, D.C. 20007

SAUDIA ARABIA
601 New Hampshire Ave., NW
Washington, D.C. 20037